# ANCIENT WISDOM FOR A MODERN DIVORCE

BY

SUSAN GOLDSTEIN AND ARNOLD GOLDSTEIN

PONCIT PUBLISHING

# ANCIENT WISDOM FOR A MODERN DIVORCE
By Susan Goldstein and Arnold Goldstein
Edited by Ken Goldstein
All content ©Goldstein Family Law
Original artwork by Travis Eberhard

PONPET PUBLISHING

# DEDICATION

To the one who is just starting the journey called
divorce, hoping this will ease the pain!

To our clients who have taught us so much.

To my leopard ladies whose creative ways
of living have been my joy and inspiration.

This book relies heavily on the teachings of two Chinese philosophers whose ancient wisdom is as relevant today as ever before. Lao Tzu, the author of the "Tao Te Ching" offers peaceful solutions to everyday problems. Sun Tzu, the author of the "Art of War" takes a more structured and militaristic approach to the same problems. They are the Yin and Yang of "Ancient Wisdom for a Modern Divorce".

# SUSI SAYS

When I was young, I loved the comic strip "Peanuts." The characters were little kids with all kinds of funny, relatable, habits Each one had a special personality quirk, easily identifiable. One, named Linus, always carried a blanket, and had the clingy needs of a typical toddler; Snoopy was the dog, always faithful; and you might remember Lucy, the bossy little girl, who excelled in telling the other kids what to do. But the one character you may not remember is the teacher. She was the adult who could corral all the kids into one room and make them pay attention. Even though she never said any real words, you still felt she had a great understanding of all the personalities in that classroom. Of all the characters in the series, she was the one I aspired to be.

Well, teaching always came naturally to me and I set out at a very early age to make that my life's work. I developed a deep love of the Spanish language and the Mexican culture from my dad, who spoke all the Romance languages, and from Mrs. Uhlir, the larger-than-life, over 300 pounds of fun, Spanish teacher I had in high school. She began and ended every class with a rousing Spanish song. How could I not want to be a teacher? I started my dream job, teaching fifth grade and Spanish in Evanston in 1963. That was the first year their schools were integrated, and we had a great group of kids, each one with their own compelling "quirk", much like the Peanuts gang, who made my chosen profession a joy. But when Kennedy was killed that November, and the world turned upside down, my life plans changed. I decided to fulfill a lifetime dream to go to Mexico for the summer with my two best friends -- and here's where fate stepped in. Just before I was ready to leave, I got fixed up with my dad's best friend's son! Little did I know how this chance meeting would *really* change my life.

My friends and I did take our trip, and from the moment I stepped foot in Cuernavaca, I was hooked. We enjoyed Mariachi bands everywhere we went, and, of course, I had to sing along with every song (thanks again, Ms. Uhlir). My friends also quickly fell in love with the language and the people. What a wonderful time we had, three girls on a dream vacation! The trip was eye opening in so many ways. We traveled by local buses (pigs, cattle, and all), slept in Iguana-infested hotels in the Yucatan (I slept in more hotel lobbies than I care to mention because the bedrooms were filled with "critters"), and met wonderful people. We met travelers from other countries who knew how to have a good time, and we partied from one end of the country to the other until we felt like natives. I was the only one of my group who spoke the language, and, as my translations were slightly off, you can imagine some uncomfortable moments. There was the time I said I was "embarazada," not knowing that meant "pregnant" instead of "embarrassed;" I couldn't understand why, all of a sudden, everyone was hovering over me.

I thought I had determined my life's path, teaching Spanish. Everything changed (as it often does) when I returned home and decided to marry my "fix up," a brilliant Atticus Finch-type lawyer whose ideas and values so closely matched my own that we knew we were bashert (meant to be) after the first 12-hour date.

Our union was more than a marriage. He needed a secretary/paralegal, I had been a crack typist since high school and was conveniently located! Together we started a law practice that has endured and prospered to this day.

I must admit that sometimes we don't know where the marriage begins, and the law practice takes over. "Law" was spoken around our dinner table, on vacations (yes, he did take his phone and laptop onto his fishing boat), and our clients became our friends and family. It was not unusual to have one client or another over for dinner almost every night or even helping me out with projects around the house! Thus, was formed our life of "living the law." There was never a dull moment!

We began our firm with corporate, business, and transactional law, but, as more and more of our clients began to divorce, we naturally fell into a family law practice that has endured for 56 years. Our partnership and our clients benefit from the fact that my husband and I don't think alike on all topics; he bounces legal strategies and ideas off of me, and I offer the "common man's" answers. In fact, I am often the one in our partnership who gets the client's crying phone call and the true "back story" first.

Beyond our exchange of ideas and strategies, he is a warrior, and I am not. He goes to court and battles for our clients with the opposing attorney, while I stay in the background providing him and the client common sense advice.

Like any famous duo, our opposite natures come into play during a case, taking a tough stance when necessary and acting with decency and respect when possible. Often, it takes this two- pronged approach to achieve the best possible outcome for our client.

So, my husband reads "The Art of War," a Twelfth century military doctrine, which many people view as the textbook on war, and I read "Tao Te Ching.", a more peaceful approach to the same ideas. These two different philosophies ultimately converge to help our clients (and even us) figure out what to do in our lives. "Conducting yourself in a peaceful" way turns out to inform you in a warlike situation. The warrior (lawyer) gathers his weapons (computers, staff, supplies), scours the landscape (reads, researches, gathers information), while the Taoist (me), stands by with common sense and non-confrontational advice!

Imagine how many hours of discussion can go into one case! It turns out that the two philosophies—one of war, one of peace-- work together to solve many situations. They are most definitely not irreconcilable.

"In the midst of chaos, there is also opportunity" (Sun Tzu). Both Lao Tzu and Sun Tzu advise that it is better to hold back and let the other party make mistakes to gain the ultimate advantage.

"The best strategy is one that delivers victory without fighting." (General Mark Petraeus). So, while Arnie is the gladiator, fighting to help his client, I'm in the background ready with a shoulder to cry on and some good, common sense advice.

This book uses ancient philosophy along

with modern thought and stories based on true incidents to encourage you to look at your own life and see where a change in thought can really make a difference.

**SUSI GOLDSTEIN**

# ARNIE SAYS

When Susi asked me to participate in her book, I was intrigued by the idea of examining our process for the last 56 years as we helped our clients find the best path out of their problems and into a better life. Susi's viewpoint is one of peaceful resolution. I see my role as a lawyer as a warrior who fights battles using the law as his weapon. As Sun Tzu says, "If you know the enemy and know yourself, you need not fear the result of a hundred battles" Just as two pieces of wood rubbed together spark a flame, our differing views help light the path through the process that we refer to as a "contested divorce.", our differing views can lead to a good solution to most problems.

Learning about "The Art of War" dramatically altered my vision of my role in a case. In fact, after Susi and I went through the process of writing down our thoughts and (really) arguing over every section, I see my lawyer role as so much more. I am in the unenviable position of having to walk two paths at once. On one hand, I need to be the cold-hearted, plotting puppeteer who controls all aspects of a case, and, on the other, I must also act as a sympa/empathetic confidant and wise grandfather! Somehow, Sun Tzu seems to give advice about warfare, and, at the same time, keeps the process moral, simple and ethical with a good outcome for all. Law school taught me the Socratic method: ask all the questions you can, gather all the knowledge you can, and conduct yourself honorably and Sun Tzu confirmed it.

The "Art of War" is a 5th-century BCE military treatise written by the Chinese strategist Sun-Tzu (aka Sunzi or Sun Wu). Covering all aspects of warfare, the book seeks to advise commanders on how to prepare, mobilize, attack, defend, and treat the vanquished. In a million years of formal law school education, you will never receive training on how to apply the "Art" to the real world any more than a law school class will teach you how to file a statutory required Appearance "as an attorney" to become formally recognized as the counsel of record.

Occasionally, a couple will have the good sense to simply decide the marriage is over; they want to go their own way, pay their appropriate share of debts, and divide assets, retirement plans, 401Ks, their residence(s), etc., fairly. If they have children, they know how they want to raise the children and how to equitably pay the children's expenses. They agree on parenting schedules, allocate parent responsibilities and decision making, and they understand that just because they are divorced, the children do not deserve to live on less of anything. The adults are divorcing each other, not their children. These are the lucky people that this book is not really written for.

We hope this book will cast some light on what "contesting" a divorce really means, and what happens to everyone involved when married folk fight over major (and minor) issues.

I admit that without the guidance of my wife (my real partner), I would be clueless in the divorce battlefield, because, as a student of the law, I tend to think that, with sufficient facts (evidence), the law will apply, and the correct results will follow automatically. That is simply not the case. Over the past 56 years, we have learned it is the artful application of a combined philosophy of the "Art of War" and "The Way of the Dao" that settles our cases and brings contested litigation to successful conclusion.

**ARNIE (the other) GOLDSTEIN**

OUR FAVORITE STORIES

## SUSI'S FAVORITE

One day, two monks set out for a temple in a valley beyond the woods. While cutting a pathway through the woods, they came across a choppy stream they needed to cross. There, standing on the bank of the stream, was a beautiful young maiden dressed in silk. She was clearly at a loss as to how to cross without getting muddy and wet.

Without thinking twice, the elder monk gestured that he would pick her up. Shocked, she agreed. He put her over his shoulder and waded across the stream to the other side. The younger monk, dismayed and uneasy by what he had witnessed, followed along.

Upon reaching the other bank, the elder monk gently put the maiden down. The maiden paid her respects and walked on. The monks then continued on their way to the temple.

As they navigated through the forest, the younger monk, still troubled by what he had seen, asked, "How could you do that? We aren't even supposed to make eye contact with women, let alone pick them up and carry them!"

Without a thought, the elder monk turned to the younger monk and said, "Oh, are you still carrying her? I put her down when I reached the other side of the stream." And with that, the elder monk turned and continued leading the way through the forest, leaving the younger monk to contemplate his words for the remainder of the journey.

Moral of the story? Are you going to carry that load forever?    LET IT GO!!

# ARNIE'S FAVORITE

I was a young attorney and Susi was still teaching during the day and running the logistics of our law practice at night, when we got a very complex case. We represented a man who had been married 9 times against a woman who had been married 11 times (twice to our client!). I had been naive enough to believe a simple Prenuptial Agreement would protect my client. The divorce began within 6 months after the couple married. The soon-to-be ex-wife had a son who was an attorney and an ex- husband who was also an attorney (and you can probably guess the rest of this description: they both specialized in "divorce practice").

The attorney selected by the wife was a former associate in the law firm in which the judge was a partner in when he was in practice. This relationship was appropriately disclosed to me, and my client and I accepted assurances from both the attorney and the judge that the prior relationship would not be a problem. I am sure that Sun Tzu was turning over in his grave at this point; we had given up ground, cut off our supply lines, our position and probably violated every other strategy in the book.

Within a month's time, we were on the wrong side of an impossible contempt citation, and, in the end, we had to go to the Appellate Court to get the judge corrected. I will never forget arguing that the wife, with her 11 marriages and a son and ex-husband who were both divorce attorneys, was endowed with more knowledge about Prenuptial Agreements than me, just recently married to my first and only wife, with not a child yet in sight. I was thrilled when the court instructed the trial judge to reverse the contempt hearing and the case then settled.

So, what is the point? Well, it's a great story; and both my client and his ex-wife went on to  marry other people. I suggested that perhaps he should talk with someone about the fact that he married everyone he dated, and then they were at fault, so he divorced them. He fired me as a business attorney and dropped me as friend for that suggestion. The point is that violating the rules of the "Art of War" such as being prepared for battle, will always bring defeat, while being prepared will never cause a loss. Moral of the story? Always remember that doing the right thing is the right way to behave.

# WHAT ABOUT...

# DON'T BE POSSESSED BY YOUR POSSESSIONS

## LAO TZU

*"Fill your house with jade and gold, and it brings insecurity. Puff yourself with honor and pride, and no one can save you from a fall."*

*"One gains by losing and loses by gaining."*

## SUN TZU

*"There are not more than five musical notes, yet the combinations of these five give rise to more melodies than can ever be heard. There are not more than five primary colours, yet in combination they produce more hues than can ever been seen. There are not more than five cardinal tastes, yet combinations of them yield more flavours than can ever be tasted."*

## ...AND...

*"Come to grips with the radical concept of 'enough is enough'."* Wayne Dyer

## THE STORY:

Of all the stories in the book, this one wins the prize! Our client, the husband, had been away on one of his "business trips." He happily arrived home, and when he opened the condo door, he was greeted by a card table set up in the elegant foyer. On the table was one glass, one plate, one spoon, one fork, one knife... you get the picture! His wife's silent comments continued as he walked through the now barren apartment; he could not even find a roll of toilet paper! When he called us, he said: "Do you think she wants a divorce?" She got what she wanted, all the contents of the apartment, and she made her point. She took everything that meant something to him -- his stuff. He was possessed by all he owned, not giving a thought to the woman who shared it with him.

She could have just served him with papers, but she took the very items he cared for the most...his material possessions. P.S.: the divorce raged on for a few years as he tried to regain the possessions.

Too much money and time was spent on minor issues while he fought for what he *thought* he wanted. I think, for her, making him struggle was just a good way to make a point; I don't think she cared for the possessions themselves.

## THE THOUGHT:

When a new divorce client comes in, we ask them "what do you want out of this?" Invariably, the list is long: dishes, glasses, furniture, etc. Most people are fixated on "stuff" at the beginning of the divorce procedure; with some of our clients, this preoccupation almost becomes obsessive as time goes on. "I want that record collection." "I want the lamp in the living room." So many divorce proceedings become bogged down by someone wanting some old thing they haven't thought of in years, just so it will stay out of the possession of the other. How important is it, really? Shouldn't the real "wish list" include the children's well-being, happiness for all, a fair settlement, and blessings on each other as they go their separate ways?

## MORE IDEAS:

Common sense must be used. We must remind the client that they will get so much more if they just give up the little item that is holding up the divorce. That picture frame? Give it up and get your freedom and happiness! That piece of china? Give it up and get your freedom and happiness! Give something up and get freedom and happiness. Seems like a small act to take to get out of an abusive or intolerable situation. What is your future happiness worth?

# ABANDON CONTROL: WHEN INACTION IS ACTION

## LAO TZU

*"Trying to control leads to ruin. Trying to grasp, we lose. Allow life to unfold naturally... There is a time for being ahead and a time for being behind."*

*"Keep your mouth shut, guard the senses and life is ever full. Open your mouth, always be busy, and life is beyond hope."*

## SUN TZU

*"Appear weak when you are strong and strong when you're weak."*

*"The Masters get the job done without moving a muscle and signify without saying a word."*

## ...AND...

*"Those who care the least about approval, get it the most.... Don't need to be right all the time... Give loving support to other, soften your glare settle your dust before you scream."* - Wayne Dyer

## THE STORY:

The wife, because of her mental and physical health issues, including alcoholism, drug abuse and child abuse, was unfit to have custody or even visitation with her children. The court would have given our client complete custody and left her with no contact. Our client, however, was a man who knew the importance of family and he had a different idea. He worked with the ex-wife to get her the counseling she needed, provided her with enough money to live on and even bought her a house a short distance from his so she could see the children. It was not easy, and it took years of failures, but eventually a successful family resulted because the husband gave up those things he could not control and worked with those he could. His generosity made it possible for the children to grow up into mentally healthy adults, the real success of this story.

## THE THOUGHT:

Practice letting go, be open minded; take the neutral ground until you can understand what's going on; do not jump in, lay back, wait, understand. Lawyers can be the guiltiest when it comes to unnecessarily grabbing control. I remember being in the judge's chambers (a very fair man), and the other lawyer just would not let anyone talk. If I tried to get a word in, he would raise his voice, argue, and generally take over the meeting. I realized I could do nothing, so that is exactly what I did. I sat back, and eventually he hung himself with his own words. The judge saw through his belligerence and made his ruling based on the real facts, not something made up by the other party.

## MORE IDEAS:

People who always must have the last word are dangerous in any negotiation. Which leads right into the next topic!

**OUR FAVORITE STORIES**

# LET EGO GO

## LAO TZU

*"Serve the needs of others and all your own needs will be fulfilled... the sage puts himself last and so ends up ahead." "Self-absorption and self-importance are vain and self-destructive."*

*"...be gentle and kind, stand by your word, govern with equity. Be timely in choosing the right moment."*

## SUN TZU

*"Know yourself and you will win all battles."*
*"You have to believe in yourself."*

## ...AND...

*"Make an attempt to reverse ego's hold on you... stop the chase and be a witness."* Wayne Dyer

*"I silence my ego... Now I call upon the Light to speak on my behalf on all occasions, so that my every word elevates my soul and all existence."* Kabbalah

## THE STORY:

We couldn't figure out why the other side was not accepting our fair offer until we found out that our own client, the wife, thought she knew best. She was negotiating on the side with the husband and had reached a deal. Her ego made her think she knew more than the experts. As it turns out, we had negotiated a better deal, but she ruined her best chance by thinking she was smarter than the paid professionals.

Another client, a man, showed his uncontrollable ego in every action he took. He could not let go, could not give up control. He called and visited the office often, usually with some new idea about the case or pleadings he thought we should file, etc. Always trying to control the situation, he jumped in at every opportunity. The worst interference came when we told him about an idea we had that would surprise his spouse and help him gain an advantage. You guessed it. He went right home and told the wife the plan, laughing at how clever he was. Thus, he spoiled any surprise we might have had and needlessly extended the case .

## THE THOUGHT:

Stop trying to control every situation, sit back, be neutral, be like a rock in the river and let things flow around you. Hear all sides and remain non-judgmental. Try to leave your ego outside the door, think in terms of what would be best for the whole family, even if it means giving up something you want. Is your preference for the good of the whole? Will giving up your desire make life better for all in the long run? This strategy does not mean the other side must always prevail, but compromise will win in the end. Lao Tzu says, "be timely in choosing the right moment." Trust that your attorney knows the right moment to ask the right question or file the right motion. Learn to wait for the right moment; timing is everything in negotiating.

**MORE IDEAS:**

The best action people going through divorce can take is to let their ego submit to that of another and retain a sense of humor. The subject of a particular piece of courtroom litigation is not always what it seems to be. The battle over $50 a month is not really a battle over money, but a battle over control. Once you recognize that concept, trying to fight some battles in the courtroom becomes a clear waste of time, and you can begin to see the reality of your situation. Stop trying to control everything. Over-management is a perfect example how your ego can hurt the outcome.

# LISTEN -- PRACTICE NOT DOING

## LAO TZU

*"He shows people how to forget what they know and what they want... If you think you've got the answers, he'll mess with your head."*

*"Practice not doing. When action is pure and selfless, everything settles into its own perfect place."*

## SUN TZU

*"Be extremely subtle, even to the point of formlessness. Be extremely mysterious, even to the point of soundlessness. Thereby you can be the director of the opponent's fate." "He who knows when he can fight and when he cannot, will be victorious."*

## ...AND...

*"Those who make peaceful revolution impossible will make violent revolution inevitable."* John F. Kennedy

## THE STORY:

I received a call from an angry client. She was beside herself because her husband had come to pick up their child, and he had not yet purchased a car seat. She stood in the driveway, ranting and raving and refusing to let him take the child for this first visitation. She called us on her cell phone. "Why can't you give him your car seat for the day?" I asked. "I hadn't thought of that", was her reply! The husband borrowed her car seat for the day and went out and bought his own. Thus, she stopped making an issue out of something she could solve easily and perhaps paving the way for a more peaceful resolution to other problems.

## THE THOUGHT:

Divorce causes an instant reaction of wanting to do something, change things, make things better. You want to get in the middle of the problem, and, like a tornado, sweep everything clean. The sense of wanting to control uncontrollable situations makes you act without thinking.

Be still. Try to let the problems swirl around you like a cloud, try to see the reality of what is going on, let yourself be like a leaf in a river. Go with the flow until you can figure out the right way. Fighting the current, trying to swim upstream, is futile. This patience is not the same as saying "don't be strong;" sometimes in standing firm, more is accomplished than in rushing to battle. In other words, be flexible; don't be a stooge or roll over unnecessarily but cooperate wherever possible to work towards a good result.

## MORE IDEAS:

The Tao teaches us that there are dualities in the universe. Light follows darkness; happiness follows sadness; good overcomes evil; relief follows pain.

In harmony with this philosophy, know that, though you may be going through a sad time, surely goodness will appear (in the form of a kind friend or a bonus at work or something as simple as a good grade on your kid's report card). Remember, "this too shall pass."(my mom) I will help to take a step back and see events from a different perspective. Relax, know that fortune will change, take the time to make yourself ready for the next situation, and be prepared to say to yourself, "I'm in a cloud, let it swirl around me, knowing that the light is just outside."

# TRUST YOUR GLADIATOR

## LAO TZU

*"The Masters don't give orders; they work with everybody else. "Peace is the prize; a victory is a disaster. "*

## SUN TZU

*"The quality of decision is like the well-timed swoop of a falcon which enables it to strike and destroy its victim."*

*"He will win who knows when to fight and when not to fight."*

## ...AND...

*"If you do something best in life, you don't really want to give that up."* Roger Federer

*"Advice is what we ask for when we already know the answer but wish we didn't."* Erica Jong

*"As a fighter, your obligation is to win."*
Yoel Romero

## THE STORY:

Our client couldn't understand why Arnie was speaking so kindly to the other attorney. The client became quite belligerent and demanded that Arnie take a stronger stance; she wanted to go in "for the kill" in the first conference. Here is what he explained to her. The bullfighter knows when to use the cape and when to use the sword. The movement of the cape is the distraction (it is not the red color because bulls are color blind) that causes the bull to charge and miss. The clever bullfighter plays with the bull until the matador is ready to use his sword. That's why the third tercio of the fight is called "muerte"...death!" If you've never been in a bullring you are missing a lot of knowledge!

## THE THOUGHT:

Throughout history, great wars have been fought and many lives lost, but perhaps the greatest battles of all are those fought between husbands and wives; rarely do these divorces end in death, but "lives" are certainly lost!

The evolution of appointing someone to represent a side in a conflict dates back to ancient times. Rather than hand to hand combat, kings decided not to endanger themselves and their armies, but instead selected a champion to represent each side.

These gladiators/knights fought to the death. After a while, the combatants got smart and decided to fight battles orally, letting a judge make the decision... and thus, the legal system was born. Today's gladiators are called lawyers. These brave souls are our combatants, fighting for our points of view so we don't have to go into the fray. In divorce, this process is especially useful in producing a civil and fair outcome for both parties.

So often, a client will sit in the office and complain unmercifully about the spouse. They did this and that; they are this and that. They will ask, "Why is my wife doing 'this or that'?" The only response the lawyer can provide is, "I don't know, I'm not in their head."

As your representative, your lawyer is bound to do what benefits you. The only way they can find that out is to speak to the other lawyer, send and receive court pleadings, and advocate for you; you are their only concern. Many times, he is asked how he can represent a person with a point of view that is directly opposite from his. The answer is, "that's what I was hired for." He will tell you, honestly, what he thinks of your position, but in the long run, your views and wishes should direct your attorney.

The hope is that you will accept your attorney's recommendations and conform to their direction. Your attorney is experienced in their field and many of their best practices have literally become second nature. You, on the other hand, are new to being a client; you have just begun this process, and you need to trust that your attorney knows what they are doing.

Often the lawyer has a "gut feeling" about a strategy or a decision, a judgment based on all his experiences in years gone by with similar cases. Chances are your lawyer knows more about the law than you do; they do it every day!

## MORE IDEAS:

Yes, there are only a few discrete scenarios in the world of divorce and, once I've worked through one or more, I have a pretty good idea of the likely outcome. So, let your gladiator/knight go into battle for you, stay out of the fray, be a good Daoist, and try to release control to someone more knowledgeable and experienced. Let go and, you will not only survive the battle, but you will also win the war.

# COOPERATION IS THE NAME OF THE GAME

## LAO TZU

*"The pieces of a chariot are useless unless they work in accordance with the whole. Playing one's part in accordance with the universe is true humility. "*

## SUN TZU

*"The supreme art of war is to subdue the enemy without fighting."*

*"Using order to deal with the disorderly, using calm to deal with the clamorous, is mastering the heart."*

## ...AND...

*"It's all right if they don't agree with you, or vice versa. Find the grain of truth in their view and know that there's no such thing as right or wrong."* Kabbalah

*"... when there is teamwork and collaboration, wonderful things can be achieved."* Mattie Stepanek

## THE STORY:

As is often the case, each party wants the same thing. In this proceeding, it was the lamp (fill in any item you choose!). The couple fought for a year over the lamp. This single dispute caused the case to go on ad nauseum, and nothing else could be accomplished. Thank goodness the husband finally went out and bought a new lamp. But what happens if an item has monetary or sentimental value? That is when it gets tough, but that is also why you have/need a gladiator!

Here is another example of a simple solution. One of our custody cases could not be settled for a long time. Meanwhile, the kids were getting older, and multiple problems cropped up. The father argued that the mother was preventing the children from talking on the phone to him when they were living with her. Court hearings were attended, and every effort was made to solve the problem. Finally, it came out that the mother's house did not have a phone charger so the kids could not charge their phones and did not want to use up their precious batteries on parental phone calls. Once a charger was purchased, the argument ended. The parties just had to be ready to cooperate to solve the problem.

## THE THOUGHT:

Most divorce attorneys handle cases for both women and men, custodial parents and non-custodial parents, and the opposite sides of any divorce case. This variety of experience gives them the unique perspective of seeing most stories from both sides. The attorney must learn how to cooperate with the other lawyer. It is interesting to see lawyers working on one side of an issue for one case and the opposite side on another case (especially in a smaller jurisdiction like ours). The lawyers may be strong adversaries in one case and cooperative "settlers" in another. Each case demands its own special handling, and the attorney must be a mediator first.

**MORE IDEAS:**

Sometimes cooperation wins the game, and the client simply must realize that cooperation is the best way to get the job done. Of course, in the heated environment of divorce, clients may not want to cooperate; they want the last little shred of whatever the other person has. When egos kick in, settlement becomes much more difficult, because if you do not cooperate on their point, your ex isn't going to want to cooperate on yours. This situation is where your attorney advises you to cooperate and hopes you take the suggestion.

# KNOWLEDGE – KNOW YOUR ENEMY

## LAO TZU

*"Those who know do not talk. Those who talk, do not know." "Close your mouth. Listen to those who are more knowledgeable. Live by silent knowing."*

## SUN TZU

*"Let your plans be dark and as impenetrable as night, and when you move, fall like a thunderbolt." "The general who wins the battle makes many calculations in his temple before the battle is fought." "If ignorant both of your enemy and yourself, you are certain to be in peril."*

## ...AND...

*"If only we were as careful about what comes out of our mouths as we are about what goes in."* Kabbalah

*"Before all else, be armed."* Niccolo Machiavelli

## THE STORY:

The coffee shop in our office building is a great place to escape for a long lunch or just to get away from the din of the legal world. That's where we met a waitress with a young son who needed to hold several jobs to get by. She was a real people person and enjoyed going to work where she could talk to the patrons. She had some legal issues and was studying all the case law she could find to help her cause. Already a college graduate, she had an innate sense of the law and she listened to the advice we gave and found out everything she could about her case. Ultimately, she came out the winner. Naturally, we enjoyed going to her restaurant just to socialize with her. We found out that she aspired to have a better career, and soon she started working as a legal secretary. Her natural ability to learn, along with a willingness to take advice and be educated, put her on a track to success in a very short time. If more people took the time to learn about what they were going through, they might go through it with better understanding and success.

## THE THOUGHT:

The sign of a highly skilled divorce lawyer is the ability to identify areas of agreement and then deal with areas of conflict. They know that you need to find agreement before you go to war. Your lawyer has been dealing with divorce proceedings a lot longer than you. Listen to their advice. Ask them to explain their strategy (he should have one; after all, they are a warrior going into battle for you). You should be able to "partner" with them, two soldiers, shoulder to shoulder, repelling the enemy and, through good strategy, winning the battle. Some clients start out by telling the lawyer what to do. They forget that they have sought professional advice because they have never been involved in divorce proceedings before, while the attorney practices this area of law every day.

During this time, the lawyer will "be there" for whatever is needed. They will not and should not, however, jump into everything. Your attorney will act only when they feel it's right.

We always advise our clients to learn the real facts and don't rely on hearsay. Make yourself as knowledgeable as possible about the actions being taken, do not be afraid to ask questions, organize your thoughts and speak with authority. Gather as much information about your spouse as possible because knowledge is power. Be truthful with your lawyer; his job will be much easier and the outcome quicker and more satisfactory.

Pretend your divorce is a basketball game, and the win depends on cooperation, especially with your own lawyer! If you act in a forthright manner, the other party is more likely to do the same and have more respect for you, improving the outcome of the case.

Get as much knowledge as you can about the divorce process so you can be a "partner" with your attorney. Question their strategic moves if you don't understand and ask them to lay out a "game plan". Once you understand their reasons you will be able to help obtain a good result.

## MORE IDEAS:

Are you contemplating a divorce? Do you know everything about your spouse? Now is the time to start collecting information such as return addresses from envelopes, which will be helpful for the attorney to know where to serve the Subpoenas.

Our most successful clients are those who respect the law, understand what is and what was happening during the marriage; these clients act as aides to the attorney by gathering information and organizing exhibits, gathering as much information as they can to help manage the case. They are also open to alternative methods, such as using special process servers, psychologists, and other experts.

These clients are a lawyer's dream because they assist the process rather than being ego- driven, always needing to be right.

## START FEELING POSITIVE AGAIN

### LAO TZU

*"Who are content needs fear no shame. Who knows to stop incurs no blame."*

### SUN TZU

*"Keep your friends close and your enemies closer."*

### ...AND...

*"The first time you win, nobody picks you; the last time you win, nobody picks you... You've just got to pick yourself."* Venus Williams

*"Tomorrow is the today we worried about yesterday!"* Sue Goldstein

*"Yesterday I was clever, so I wanted to change the world. Today I am wise, so I am changing myself."* Rumi

"I yam what I yam and that's all that I yam!" Popeye

## THE STORY:

Mona walked in the office looking like a dragged out, worn down person. Her demeanor was that of someone who had been beaten, literally. She was crying, feeling like the weight of the world was on her shoulders. All through the first part of her case, this behavior continued.

Soon, the case started going her way, and gradually I noticed changes were taking place. She started going out a little, fixed herself up and began having a better self-view. This attitude adjustment gave her more confidence, and she was able get a good job, which reinforced her new persona even more.

When the divorce was almost over, a new woman walked into the office; cool, confident, beautifully dressed and looking like she felt... powerful!

## THE THOUGHT:

For many clients, going through a divorce is a solitary event. Even those clients who have support can, at times, feel lonely, hopeless, and, in general, sorry for themselves. Unchecked thoughts can spiral into depression and worse. The best advice is to get out and get help. Professional therapy is always a good idea, but assistance is all around us in many forms. Do you have a religious group nearby? Go to a service. Join a group or activity that interests you to meet people and feel the support of a community. What about resurrecting an old hobby? Do you like to dance? Find your nearest Arthur Murray dance studio or any music venue and go! You would be surprised what at night of dancing can do to boost your ego!

**MORE IDEAS**:

You thought you were a good person before all this craziness started. You were good looking, capable, and accomplished before you met "Mr. Wonderful." Spend a quiet minute and try to go back to that time to remember your former existence. Try to regain those feelings of self- worth so you can bolster your confidence for the attacks that are likely to come. As self-help guru Wayne Dyer says, "Change your mind, change your life!"

# FORGIVE OTHERS; FORGIVE YOURSELF

## LAO TZU

*"The journey of a thousand miles begins with one step."*

## SUN TZU

*"Even the finest sword plunged into saltwater will eventually rust."*

## ...AND...

*"But what I learned to do many years ago was to forgive myself. It is very important for every human being to forgive herself or himself because if you live, you will make mistakes- it is inevitable. But once you do and you see the mistake, then you forgive yourself and say, 'Well, if I'd known better, I'd have done better,' that's all."*

Maya Angelou

*"Be like a tree and let the dead leaves drop."* Rumi

*"Forgiveness is a perpetual journey. There are many bridge crossings. Each restores a bit more of what you have lost."* Rabbi Karyn D. Kedar

## THE STORY:

An important family occasion was in the near future. Mona, the second wife and stepmother, thought of all the horrible scenarios that could take place at what should be a happy time. The first wife was not an easy person to get along with, Mona could predict a bad outcome with all the family and friends attending the party.

Mona knew that the occasion could either be happy or tragically sad for the children and her husband at the hands of this difficult person. Gathering all her strength, she contacted the first wife and asked for a meeting. When they met, the stepmother spoke about how the two of them could "make or break" this happy family occasion and suggested ways that they could cooperate to make the event go well.

The day arrived, and Mona steeled herself to walk into a room full of her enemies, but being the classy person she is, she put a smile on her face and said, "I'm not going to let anything ruin this day for my family,"

To her relief and amazement, she encountered a room full of good will; the first wife worked with her and the relatives were gracious. The two women even made a speech together. This event could have gone horribly awry with nothing but bad feelings in place of what should have been a happy occasion. So, leave your ego at the door, forgive, even if it is only for one day, and then try compassion and empathy in other parts of your life... you will be pleasantly surprised.

Mona, who is a beautiful, gracious person, knew right from the beginning of her marriage that she was responsible for the family holidays, and she always worked closely with the first wife, sharing cooking, decorating, and other ways to participate. The first wife was always a welcome guest at her table and the two women have formed a friendship, allowing the whole family to thrive because of this important relationship.

## THE THOUGHT:

There are forces at work in the world that affect what you think and do. It is up to you to make or break any given situation. Only you can make an event or an outing go smoothly. Through your peaceful actions, you can demonstrate to others how they should behave, and perhaps their anger can be abated. The vibe you send out comes back at you, so stay calm, cool, and decent. Forgiveness is a like a narrow bridge; sometimes you meet face to face in the middle and one person must step aside temporarily to let the other pass, or both might fall off!

## KEEP COOL

## LAO TZU

*"Hold on to the center. Man was made to sit quietly and find the truth within."*

*"Trying to understand is like straining through muddy water. Have the patience to wait! Be still and allow the mud to settle."*

## SUN TZU

*"He who knows when he can fight and when he cannot, will be victorious. "Sweat more during peace; bleed less during war."*

## ...AND...

*"Before you speak, listen. Before you write, think. Before you spend, earn. Before you invest, investigate. Before you criticize, wait. Before you pray, forgive. Before you quit, try. Before you retire, save. Before you die, give."* William Arthur Ward

*"In the blackest of your moments, wait with no fear."*
Rumi

## THE STORY:

Mona was a typical Lucy character, never able to keep her mouth shut, always jumping in with criticism or the last word. Mickey was just the opposite, always holding back, staying cool and not reacting to his wife's vile attitude. It took their young daughter to say, "Mom, why don't you let dad have a chance to talk sometime?" to make Mona realize how strident she had become. Of course, it was too late, because Mickey already had "other arrangements" and Mona. was served with papers.

## THE THOUGHT:

It is so easy to judge, to point the finger; it's always the other guy's fault. Try to remain objective and leave judgmental thoughts out of the process. Yes, your spouse has his/her problems, but those concerns are not the issue right now. You are getting rid of that problem, you are moving on to a better place; focus on a good path forward, leave criticism outside, and try to think objectively.

## MORE IDEAS:

By this time, you realize that one of our main themes is "keep your cool." Don't always speak or jump into the argument; lay back and wait. Give that ego a rest. Be like the tiger that waits in the bushes for the right time to pounce, or the warrior who stays in the background until the right time to attack. More wars (and relationships) have been lost by poor timing and the parties' inability to wait for the proper time to act or speak.

# ALWAYS HAVE A "PLAN B"; PLANS "C" AND "D"

## LAO TZU

*"If you are rigid and unyielding, you might as well be dead. If you are soft and flexible, you are truly alive."*

## SUN TZU

*"Be extremely subtle, even to the point of formlessness. Be extremely mysterious, even to the point of soundlessness. Thereby you can be the director of the opponent's fate."*

**...AND...**

*"When life doesn't go according to plan, roll with it."*
Kabbalah

*"We would like to live as we once lived, but history will not permit it. "Change is the law of life. And those who look only to the past or present are certain to miss the future".* John F. Kennedy

*"The only thing certain in life is change."* Momma Cele

## THE STORY:

Having a "Plan B" provides consolation and comfort during a hard time. If you know there is something better waiting for you when the darkness is over, it is easier to get through the hard times.

Mona endured an abusive situation for years, coming to the edge of divorce many times, but never able to take the final step. She did have a plan, however. She went to school quietly for years, finally getting a degree that enabled her to get a part time job. She set up a second bank account and eventually saved enough to make her move. It took a lot of courage for her to make such a dramatic change. There were many risks involved, including fear of a physical attack, but she felt the outcome was worth it for her and her children.

## THE THOUGHT:

"The only thing certain in life is change." This phrase was the watchword of Mamma Cele who managed to make it through many crises in her life, including escaping the Cossacks in Russia, the Depression, deaths, and marital problems. She always was able to get through the dark days because she knew that "this too shall pass;" there is always calm at the end of the storm". If you can focus on the longer term, you can get through a crisis by knowing it won't last forever.

So, too, in divorce, the days may look dark and angry, but, after they pass, there will be light and peace.

## MORE IDEAS:

Choose change: Change is a choice. Not an easy choice, because it really takes work to turn your negativity around but keep making the choice and you will see a shift happen. Today, connect with your intention to change. The more you choose activities and people that support your forward movement, the stronger you will become.

# WHAT ABOUT THE CHILDREN?

## LAO TZU

*"Few things in this world are as important as raising children."*

*"Live in accordance with the nature of things... be gentle and kind, stand by your word... move in harmony with the present moment... know the truth of just what to do."*

## SUN TZU

*"There is no instance of a nation benefitting from a prolonged warfare."*

## ...AND...

*"It is easier to build strong children than to repair broken men."* Frederick Douglass

*"Teach thy tongue to say, 'I do not know,' and thou shalt progress."* Maimonides

*"Today, little by little, learn to be more forgiving. Look to where you can come from a place of help, rather than judgment."* Kabbalah.

## THE STORY:

"$8.50" *or* "IT'S THE FINAL STRAW." The woman who called the office that day was very sure of her decision. She had put up with her husband's many faults, including abuse and infidelity, because of the children. She had not wanted to give up, and she thought she could just keep up the charade.

They lived separately, and she was in constant misery for many years, but she could not find the will to move on. Then one day she needed to pay for her kid's haircut; she asked her husband for half of the charge, and his "no" was the final straw! "$8.50" changed her life! She filed immediately!

Many times, the spouse who does not have physical custody of the child(ren) thinks the children can get along on much less money than when they were living as a family. The supporting spouse does not want to give enough to continue the lifestyle the child has become accustomed to. Often the supporting spouse feels they deserve to keep on with their _own_ lifestyle to the detriment of the rest of the family.

## THE THOUGHT:

The parent who leaves the home, gets an apartment, and begins to lead a separate life sometimes forgets that they left behind a situation at home that needs to continue. There are still bills to pay, the children and the custody spouse need basics (and luxuries), and food needs to be put on the table.

The supporting parent needs to understand reality and cannot expect the family to reduce its living expenses while the non-custodial spouse gets to have a new life.

## MORE IDEAS:

How petty to withhold money for a haircut for your child! This miserliness shows the true character of a person, evidenced by his willingness to use his child as a weapon against his wife. Stinginess is probably the most common behavior we see. One partner wants to get even with the other and thinks that by withholding a simple need, he will win. This action paves the way for the other partner to do the same, and before they know it, both husband and wife are in court, each paying for their lawyer's time. Think about the consequences of your actions!

## KNOW YOURSELF

### LAO TZU

*"I choose the experience I am feeling."*

*"You make a difference. Choose something to do, one act of unkindness spirals outward. You'll become what you think about, let go. Don't control, relax."*

### SUN TZU

*"Know the enemy, know yourself, and victory is never in doubt, not in a hundred battles."*

### ...AND...

*"You have brains in your head. You have feet in your shoes. You can steer yourself any direction you choose. You're on your own. And you know what you know. And YOU are the guy who'll decide where to go."* Dr. Seuss

*"The lighter you allow within you, the brighter the world you live in will be."* Shakti Gawain

*"Forgive yourself."* Rabbi Karyn D. Kedar

## THE STORY:

Most people tend to wallow in their misery, and they tend to stay there for way too long. When we met Mona. she was surviving her divorce, barely, and faced post-decree problems. Her nonworking time was taken up with all the court problems, and she had little energy or desire to do anything else. Being the mother that I am, while Arnie was spending all his time battling the other lawyer, I had a chance to talk to her. During the conversations, I found out that she loved to cook. In the days that followed, we were treated to many wonderful things from her kitchen. We suggested she use her cooking skills to move away from the sadness of her life. Sure enough, she took classes at night until she earned a degree and eventually opened her own cooking school.

Sometimes doing something for yourself, is the best investment.

## THE THOUGHT:

First, remember, this is your experience; live it, realize it, embrace it, and, as your understanding expands, so will your acceptance. It's so easy to "lose yourself" at this fragile time. All your thoughts are on the divorce procedure. "Where did I go wrong"? "How will I get along?" Do yourself a favor each day by doing something for yourself; go to a movie, take a walk and look at your surroundings, take up a hobby, anything to get you out of the reality you're in. If you can't find an hour, find one minute, and hopefully expand that time each day. Something as simple as just stepping outside on a beautiful day will change your perspective. Close your eyes for 5 minutes and think about how things will be different when you open them. Try to stay in the present and not worry or be afraid of the future.

Do what you must do to get through. Lighten up, do something silly, play like a kid again, see what it's like to suspend responsibility for an hour, a day.

## MORE IDEAS:

Nobody can go through an emotional experience like divorce without a strong support group. Many are fortunate to have a close family member or best friend who can listen and help. But those allies are not enough. They might be giving advice out of sympathy, or not wanting to hurt your feelings, or just plain lack of knowledge about such a personal subject. Here is where your professional comes in. Find a great therapist, psychiatrist or social worker who can guide you through these rocky waters.

Very early in a case, I will give the name of an appropriate therapy person to my new client, and hopefully they will work together throughout the case and beyond. People who take this advice and work with a good therapist invariably do better through the divorce process. If you are not happy with the therapist you choose, work to find one who is compatible with you and your feelings.

## BE A GRACIOUS WINNER

### LAO TZU

*"After you have attained your purpose you must not parade your success, you must not boast of your ability, you must not feel proud; you must rather regret that you had not been able to prevent the war."*

### SUN TZU

*"Build your opponent a golden bridge to retreat across." "For them to perceive the advantage of defeating the enemy, they must also have their rewards."*

### ...AND...

*"You must leave a corner of your field, and whatever falls off, the gleanings should be left for the poor, and to the stranger..."* (Leviticus 23:22)

*"If you can react the same way to winning and losing, that's a big accomplishment."* Chris Evert

*"You learn how to be a gracious winner and an outstanding loser."* Joe Namath

*"You gotta give a little, take a little, let your poor heart break a little".* Jimmy Durante

## THE STORY:

When you're settling up the divorce and dividing the house, think about what you really need. Are you taking that mirror because you really need/want it or just because the other person likes/wants it? Could you consider leaving all the silverware, so your spouse has a complete set, or do you really need that one spoon, fork, and knife? Our client was gracious, gave his wife what she wanted, left without many marital possessions, but he gained a new life, free of any encumbrances from the old. He got to buy new stuff, set up a great apartment, and she was happy to let him go.

## THE THOUGHT:

Okay, so you have gotten your divorce, you feel you have had the best outcome, you are the big winner. Leave it at that. You have a whole new life to look forward to; leave your victory on the battle ground and go forward with new confidence to make the best life possible for you, your children and, yes, even that miserable spouse. He wants a lamp, fine, you want a new life; he wants a bookshelf, fine, you want a new life! Get it? We always say that a sign of a successful divorce is that each party (and the lawyers) think they won!

## FINAL THOUGHTS:

The theme running through our book. It is the watchword of self-help groups, psychologists, and guidance counselors... let go! Many people add "and let God" to that statement. Think about it.

Let go of the past so you can go forward and live a peaceful, creative, well-spent life. There are many places to get help so you can go through the process of "letting go" with confidence and security. In our area, there are many social service agencies that support people as they navigate the stormy waters of post-marital stress.

## MORE IDEAS:

Choose change: Change is a choice. Not an easy choice, because it really takes work to turn your negativity around but keep making the choice and you will see a shift happen. Today, connect with your intention to change. The more you choose activities and people that support your forward movement, the stronger that part of you will become.

Whether you are in an abusive situation, alcoholic and dangerous relationship, or there are children's issues, there is an agency in your area ready to help: religious centers, court systems, schools, hospitals, police departments or on the Internet. Do not be afraid to ask, there is always an "angel" around to help!

NOTE: We intend this book to be used as a "workbook" to help you go through this difficult life event. Make notes in the margin, role play the stories, discuss it with your friends. You'd be surprised how many people are going through the same things and are willing to talk about it.

# THANKS

To Arn and Ken for their patience, expertise and respect
for my vision and the hours of arguing, discussing and
rewriting at every opportunity.... all over the house, before,
during and after every meal.

To my family who took the time to read and make excellent
suggestions and comments.

To Judy for her enthusiastic support and endless positivity.

To Sue, my fearless editor and friend, for always seeing
and speaking the truth.

To Bobbie the best storyteller.

To our clients who continue to teach us what we
should and should not do.

To Charles Le Chien, the wisest one of all!

Time past is irreplaceable.

Who knows what tomorrow will bring?

But today, today is precious.

Give yourself permission to enjoy today.

Take a mental snow day.

Do something that gives you pleasure.

*"Today, little by little, learn to be more forgiving. Look to where you can come from a place of help, rather than judgment."* Kabbalah.

Made in the USA
Monee, IL
03 May 2021